W9-BSL-645

A Primary Source Investigation of
THE UNDERGROUND
RAILROAD

**Viola Jones
and Philip Wolny**

rosen publishing's
rosen
central

SAYVILLE LIBRARY

Published in 2016 by The Rosen Publishing Group, Inc.
29 East 21st Street, New York, NY 10010

Copyright © 2016 by The Rosen Publishing Group, Inc.

First Edition

All rights reserved. No part of this book may be reproduced in any form
without permission in writing from the publisher, except by a reviewer.

Library of Congress Cataloging-in-Publication Data

Jones, Viola.
A primary source investigation of the Underground Railroad/Viola Jones
and Philip Wolny.
     pages cm.—(Uncovering American history)
Includes bibliographical references and index.
ISBN 978-1-4994-3517-7 (library bound)
1. Underground Railroad—Juvenile literature. 2. Fugitive slaves—United
States—History—19th century—Juvenile literature. 3. Antislavery
movements—United States—History–19th century—Juvenile literature.
4. Underground Railroad—Sources—Juvenile literature. 5. Antislavery
movements—United States—History—19th century—Sources—Juvenile
literature. I. Wolny, Philip. II. Title.
E450.J716 2016
973.7'115—dc23

                                              2014043866

Manufactured in thc United States of America

CONTENTS

In the decades before the Civil War effectively ended the institution of slavery in
the United States, many people risked their
lives to rescue southern African Americans
from the shackles of slavery and shepherd
them to the safety of the northern states and
Canada.

Escape was dangerous business. Those
who helped slaves leave their harrowing conditions faced fines and imprisonment. Those
slaves who were discovered fleeing faced
much worse upon return to their owners. That
is why it was necessary to create a secret network known as the Underground Railroad to
move slaves northward to safety.

The Underground Railroad was not a true
railroad but rather a network of people and
places. Those who worked on the "railroad"
were known as conductors. They harbored
fugitive slaves in secret, then helped them
connect to the next "station," where another
conductor would help them, on and on, northward, until they were safe.

Thousands of slaves made the journey
under cover of night by foot, or stowed
away on a ship, or—in one instance—mailed

An escaped slave attempts to cross the Ohio River.
Underground Railroad stations ushered fleeing slaves
northward to safety.

in a crate. They were hidden away in attics, barns, and cellars until it was safe to move on. Women disguised themselves as men, and those African Americans who could passed themselves off as white, all to avoid attracting attention and detection.

Once free, many became agents of the railroad to help other slaves reach freedom. Some became famous by publishing accounts of their lives and traveling the northern states to speak against slavery. They were instrumental in spreading the word about the horrors of slavery. They stirred emotions in the North and helped create a great divide between the northern and southern states. This culminated in the Civil War (1861–1865), which finally made slavery illegal in all of the states.

CHAPTER ONE

LIFE, LIBERTY, AND THE PURSUIT OF HAPPINESS

In declaring independence from Great Britain in 1776, the Founding Fathers of the United States of America claimed that "all men are created equal, that they are endowed by their Creator with certain unalienable Rights, that among these are Life, Liberty and the pursuit of Happiness." These words are the cornerstone of the American republic. Yet for nearly a century following America's independence, they would prove to be ironic. For many living in the young nation, freedom and equality were rights that didn't apply to them.

A PECULIAR INSTITUTION

Although the new nation was committed to equality and liberty, it denied the most basic freedoms to many of its residents. Throughout the seventeenth, eighteenth, and first half of the nineteenth centuries, slavery was practiced in the United States. Africans were kidnapped from their homes and villages by slave traders; placed into crowded, disease-ridden ships and brought to America; and sold as slaves in public markets to landowners and merchants. This buying and selling of human beings was considered to be legal. In the pre–Civil War years, gaining a slave's freedom meant breaking the law. Freedom was something for which slaves would have to fight long and hard. Yet they would not fight alone. From free blacks, to former slaves, to Quakers and other white American abolitionists, the fight against slavery became a crusade to make America live up to its promises and ideals.

Many southerners did not like to even use the term "slavery," referring to the practice as "our peculiar institution." This meant something that was distinctive to the South. Although the term was too indelicate for them, the practice of slavery was not. Millions of black Americans were in bondage, working as slaves on farms in the southern United States, raising many crops. One of the most important crops was cotton. Many proslavery forces believed that the South's power and wealth depended on the free labor that slaves provided. Many in the nation, particularly in the North but also a good number in the South, opposed slavery. They thought that no human being should own another and take away his or her liberty or basic human dignity. Some slaves were often treated no better than animals and were whipped, beaten, and even killed for minor offenses.

THE MOVEMENT TO ABOLISH SLAVERY

Though unpopular at first, an antislavery movement began to grow in strength and numbers. These antislavery activists were called abolitionists. "Abolition" means to end or destroy. Abolitionists wanted to outlaw slavery everywhere in the United States. Abolitionists had early success in the

Illustrations of the American Anti-Slavery Almanac for 1840.

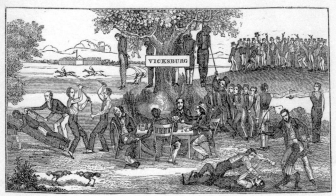

"Our Peculiar Domestic Institutions."

Northern Hospitality—New-York nine months law. [The Slave steps out of the Slave State, and his chains fall. A Free State, with another chain, stands ready to re-enslave him.]

Burning of McIntosh at St. Louis, in April, 1836.

Showing how slavery improves the condition of the female sex.

The Negro Pew, or "Free" Seats for black Christians.

Mayor of New-York refusing a Carman's license to a colored Man.

Servility of the Northern States in arresting and returning fugitive Slaves.

Selling a Mother from her Child.

Hunting Slaves with dogs and guns. A Slave drowned by the dogs.

"Poor things, 'they can't take care of themselves.'"

Mothers with young Children at work in the field.

A Woman chained to a Girl, and a Man in irons at work in the field.

Branding Slaves.

Cutting up a Slave in Kentucky.

Paid. Unpaid.

The collection of images depicting slave life published on this 1840 broadside by the American Anti-Slavery Society was intended to inform the public about the horrors of slavery.

North, where attitudes were more liberal and progressive and the economy was not dependent upon slave labor. Between 1777 and 1804, all northern states abolished slavery. Millions of African American men and women in the southern states, however, remained captives.

Abolitionism slowly gained supporters. Many prominent religious and political leaders, as well as influential business-men and society women, spoke against slavery at meetings in cities, towns, and villages in the North. Even though the northern states had abolished slavery, it was still dangerous to speak one's mind on the subject. Abolitionists were sometimes lynched by angry mobs. Many in the North who had close business ties to agricultural production in the South thought of slavery as necessary to their economic well being.

Some abolitionists joined forces and started their own societies, or clubs, to help spread their message and further their cause. Many of these societies began their own newspapers dedicated to abolition, like William Lloyd Garrison's the *Liberator*. They spoke in churches and halls throughout the country in an effort to end support

The Fugitive Slave Law was condemned on this 1850 Massachusetts abolitionist poster.

WILLIAM LLOYD GARRISON AND THE ABOLITIONIST PRESS

While some abolitionists threw their energies into the Underground Railroad, others were taking on the equally important and difficult task of convincing Americans that slavery was a great evil. The popular press provided the perfect platform for antislavery appeals to the public. In 1831, William Lloyd Garrison, a white newspaper editor, printed the first issue of his antislavery newspaper, the *Liberator*, which he published every week for the next twenty-five years.

Garrison reached out to Boston's black community and to blacks nationwide. As a result, most of his first subscribers were African Americans. At the time, Garrison's views were considered extreme, even though he sought change through nonviolent means and called for a voluntary, nationwide rejection of slavery, rather than forcing people to abandon slavery by outlawing it.

The efforts of the abolitionists called attention to the brutal plight of the slaves and rallied support against slavery. Through their courageous efforts—protests, speeches, sermons, editorials, political campaigning and debate, hiding or rescuing fugitives—abolitionists paved the way for the end of slavery in the United States. Their struggle would be long and hard fought, however, and much blood would be shed along the way.

of slavery through moral persuasion. Moderates, those who believed that change should be gradual, thought that changing people's minds was the first step to changing society.

DEVELOPMENT OF THE UNDERGROUND RAILROAD

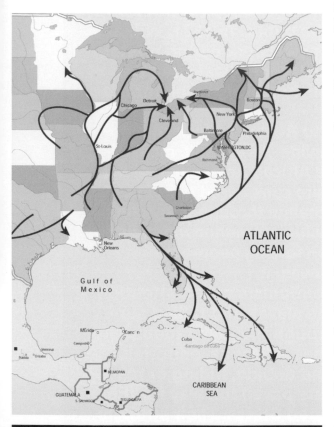

This map depicts the routes of the Underground Railroad. Arrows from slave states direct northward to free states and Canada, and southward to the Caribbean.

Other abolitionists, however, thought that change was not coming quickly enough. Believing that a more active approach was required, they decided to take matters into their own hands. Some traveled to the South and attempted to free slaves by helping them flee their masters. For these escapes to be successful, there needed to be a way to safely and secretly transport escaped slaves to the North. Fugitive slaves were sometimes hidden in the homes of people who believed it was their moral duty to help their fellow human beings. Slowly, a loose network of "safe homes" developed, dedicated to helping fugitive slaves escape to freedom.

At first, this escape system had no official name. Many of those helping the slaves escape worked in small, isolated groups and had little contact with other "stations" on the route. Plans to help fugitives were made by word of mouth. Rumors would spread, for example, that a certain person in a certain town would help. Hearing this, an abolitionist who lived a few towns away would send fugitives to that person. Sometimes a guide helped them travel between safe houses. Other times they had to fend for themselves.

As abolitionism grew, more and more people became involved in the network and began to communicate with each other. It became known that certain towns were abolitionist hotspots. Many of these were in midwestern states such as Michigan, Ohio, Indiana, and Illinois. These states are near the Great Lakes that border Canada, which was a popular destination. By the early nineteenth century, Canada had ruled that slaves who left their masters were free and could not be forcibly returned to them. Meanwhile, other abolitionist groups interested in helping slaves escape to freedom began to form in New York, Philadelphia, and Boston. The tracks for the Underground Railroad were being laid.

CHAPTER TWO

TRAVELING ON THE UNDERGROUND RAILROAD

The only thing that separated the slave South from the free North was the Mason-Dixon Line, an invisible boundary between Pennsylvania and Maryland. But gaining freedom wasn't as simple as crossing that line. Even if slaves managed to break free from their masters and step onto northern soil, they had to worry about being captured by fugitive-slave hunters. Captured slaves who were returned to their masters met with severe punishment.

The stakes were high. The resourceful agents of the Underground Railroad had to use secret codes, maps, midnight journeys, and deception to free slaves and sneak them to the safety of free states and Canada.

THE RAILROAD AS A METAPHOR

By the 1830s, trains were gaining popularity as a means of transporting goods and people. So it was only natural for the Underground Railroad to adopt the terms of this new, exciting form of American transportation to describe its operations and members.

Those who escorted slaves between safe houses— whether on foot, by boat, by horse and wagon, or even on actual locomotives—were known as conductors. The homes and businesses where fugitives hid were called stations or depots. The homeowners were known as stationmasters. Individuals who contributed money to the cause were sometimes called stockholders. Important railroad agents were often given mock titles. For example, Indiana resident Levi Coffin, who with his wife, Catharine,

Allen Walls peers from behind a fake bookshelf that once hid slaves at his house in Lakeshore Township, Ontario, Canada. Walls's great-grandfather, John Freeman Walls, turned the house into an Underground Railroad museum in 1846, one year after he escaped from bondage in South Carolina.

helped some two thousand slaves reach freedom, was sometimes referred to as president of the Underground Railroad. As news of the railroad's expanding operations spread throughout the slave states, people began to whisper about "catching the next train" north.

Some conductors, like Harriet Tubman, an African American, would travel to the plantations themselves and escort the slaves personally. Other times, slaves received only an obscure message or rumor telling them where to go. All along the railroad, slaves would move 10 to 20 miles (16 to 32 kilometers) a night. In the South, they often had to stay in abandoned barns, caves, or other remote, secret places. Upon reaching the North, the homes and businesses of the abolitionists were their stations and depots.

THE PERILS OF TRAVELING FROM STATION TO STATION

Fugitives riding the Underground Railroad traveled north slowly. Most routes of the railroad, whether passing through Ohio, Indiana, Pennsylvania, or New York, eventually led to the Great Lakes. There, fugitives could be taken by boat to Canada, the only truly safe refuge for escaped slaves in North America.

Stations were often no more than 20 miles (32 km) apart. This was considered the longest distance that fugitives could cover in a night, especially if they were on foot. Many times, a group of fugitives split up and stayed in separate shelters to make it harder for slave hunters to track them. Agents of the railroad found creative ways to stall or mislead these bounty hunters.

In Henrietta Buckmaster's *Flight to Freedom*, the author relates the case of an unidentified tavern keeper in Bloomfield, Ohio. One day a family of slaves came to his door. He fed them and let them rest. Soon, the slave hunters arrived, asking if runaways had been spotted. The tavern keeper replied that he had seen them pass by and that they were about a mile (1.6 km) up the road. This stationmaster suggested that the men should stay the night; they could easily capture the fugitives in the morning.

Every one of the slave hunters overslept the next morning when the tavern keeper failed to wake them early. Upon rising late, the hunters were impatient to get back to the chase. But the key to the stables where their horses had been placed for the night was missing, and it took some time to find it. Then, coincidentally, the horses each had a horseshoe missing. When the slave hunters finally found a blacksmith to reshoe the horses, the fugitives had placed many miles between themselves and the bounty hunters. They were well on their way to the next station, safe—at least temporarily—from further harassment.

THE IMPORTANCE OF DISGUISE

Successful slave escapes depended on the use of disguises. Blacks who had escaped earlier and returned to the South to help others flee often posed as slaves to attract less attention. A black man dressed himself in the clothes of a mourning widow, with a black veil covering his face. A young black woman could cut her hair short, put on men's clothes, and pose as a laborer. These disguises and costumes would help the fugitives pass through society without arousing much attention or curiosity.

White agents of the Underground Railroad who went south had easier ways to cover their activities. John Fairfield was a white agent of the railroad who employed disguises in his work to help runaways. An attractive, charismatic man, Fairfield looked like the typical southern gentleman. He often used wigs and makeup to disguise himself and the fugitives in his charge. At one point, during a trip near Cincinnati, he disguised himself and twenty-eight fugitives as mourners in a funeral procession. He had even hired a hearse to complete the illusion.

COMMUNICATION ON THE RAILROAD

Since the activities of the Underground Railroad could not be spoken of or written about freely, secret codes were devised so that agents and slaves alike could communicate escape plans. For example, the word "shepherds" meant that a conductor on the railroad was in the area. On the way north, news that "the wind blows from the south today" warned everyone that slave hunters were nearby.

Some say that one of the cleverer methods of communication was the use of quilts. Since most slaves had been deprived of education and few could read, other means of communication were necessary. As such, quilts were said to be used to alert slaves on how to escape and where to go. Specific quilt patterns may have conveyed certain types of information. The quilts were draped out in the open for slaves to see—like wash hanging on a clothesline to dry.

Some of the images' alleged meanings were relatively clear. A quilted sailboat might mean that a boat was available in a nearby river. A monkey wrench pattern might mean it was time to collect the tools needed for an escape.

Slave Quilts

The Slaves used their African designs in the applique quilts that they made and the sense of color and style in their pieced quilts was also inspired by African tradition. A slave might be given a blanket once every three years, quilts were a necessity. These women knew from their mothers how to make vegetable dyes and could turn rough slave cloth into every color of the rainbow. They used worn clothes and scraps from the mistress of the house. Few of these quilts survived, they were used until they wore out. As the abolitionist movement grew in the north quilts were sold to raise money for the abolitionist cause. The story that some patterns in quilts were used to pass secret messages in the underground railroad network remains uncertain, however the legend has now become part of American history.

Quilts may have been used to send coded messages that helped fugitives along the Underground Railroad. Because quilts were commonly hung out to dry, these messages could be out in plain sight, without arousing the suspicion of plantation owners.

BOX BROWN

One of the more astounding slave escapes was undertaken by Henry "Box" Brown. Born a slave in Virginia, Brown was sent to work in a tobacco factory. His wife and children toiled as slaves on a nearby plantation. When they were sold to a plantation in North Carolina, Brown knew he would never see his family again. He resolved to escape from the bonds of slavery.

The slave Henry "Box" Brown achieved his freedom by being shipped in a cargo box to Philadelphia.

In 1849, Brown had a friend pack him into a box addressed to the Philadelphia Anti-Slavery Society. With only a little bit of water, some crackers, and a tool with which he poked airholes into the box, Brown was shipped via wagon, boat, and railroad to Philadelphia. There, James McKim and other abolitionists opened the box and were delighted to find Brown alive.

Brown published a memoir detailing his escape and became a minor celebrity. With his renown came danger of being recaptured, so he moved to England, where he worked in show business.

Other images were more obscure. A song that became popular later ("Follow the Drinking Gourd") is said to have contained information on how to escape to the free North. The gourd (a container for water) was a poetic reference to the stars of the Big Dipper, which pointed to the North Star. Thus, the drinking gourd (dipper) symbolized using the North Star like a compass to guide them at night to Canada. These slave quilts were said to have been a secret way of directing runaways to where they needed to go while relaying information about possible dangers ahead.

The ways that agents and passengers of the Underground Railroad communicated with each other seemed limitless. A stationmaster in one town, for instance, told runaways that they would find the next town's station by looking for a candle lit in the third floor of a particular house. Or perhaps a white handkerchief would be tied to a tree at the gate of a stationmaster's property. The chimney of a railroad station might be identified by the white bricks used in its construction. In the middle of the night, conductors who worked with Levi and Catharine Coffin would gently rap at their door to signal that fugitives had arrived. Passwords were often used to identify those who were friendly to the cause. A certain handshake between a conductor and a stationmaster would also be a signal that the other was to be trusted.

MOTHER HUBBARD'S CUPBOARD AND OTHER PLACES TO HIDE

In the various stations along the way, agents of the Underground Railroad found ways of making their homes and businesses effective and often clever hiding places for their illegal guests. Secret compartments were built where slaves could stay for days, weeks, and even months. Fake walls were installed. Holes were dug in the shafts of wells. Churches and abandoned buildings were converted to safe places where slaves were harbored.

Tunnels and other escape routes were used to move fugitives quickly and all but invisibly. One well-known Ohio abolitionist, Colonel William Hubbard, had a tunnel dug from his barn to the edge of nearby Lake Erie. Boat captains would wait there to usher runaways across the lake and into Canada. In Underground Railroad mythology, this station was sometimes known as Mother Hubbard's Cupboard. Sometimes even the peculiar way a house was built made it a surprisingly effective station. In Pennsdale, Pennsylvania, an abolitionist named Edward Morris owned the Bull's Tavern. It was also known as the House of Many Stairs because there were seven staircases in the two-story

Visitors to the Lewelling Quaker House Underground Railroad Museum in Salem, Iowa, can crawl into this slave hideaway hidden under the house's floorboards. (The handrails are not original.)

building. Secret panels at the top of each staircase hid the fugitives, who could quickly disappear behind them should slave hunters suddenly arrive at the tavern.

Some of these hiding places can still be seen today. They are a physical reminder that, for many Americans, freedom came at great risk. Not only were escaping slaves subject to recapture and punishment, but those agents of the Underground Railroad who helped them along the way were putting a lot on the line. White agents could be fined or put in jail for aiding and abetting. Black agents in the North risked being caught and sold into slavery despite their freedom. And those in the South risked their lives.

CHAPTER THREE

STORIES OF THE UNDERGROUND RAILROAD

In spite of the very serious risks to all involved, more Americans joined the abolitionist movement every year. For them, the possibility of ending slavery outweighed the risks to their property and safety. The Underground Railroad was one of the earliest, most important organized interracial efforts in U.S. history. Black and white, men and women, rich and poor—all came together to rid the country of the evils of slavery and achieve a society that was truly free. Their stories—a few of which are told in the following sections—help us understand the significance of the Underground Railroad.

"THE MOSES OF HER PEOPLE"

Harriet Ross was born a slave, sometime around 1820, in the slave state of Maryland. (A baby born to slaves became the property of their master.) As a young child, Harriet suffered brutal whippings. When she was twelve, a white overseer clubbed her in the head after she refused to tie up a fellow slave who had tried to escape. When she was twenty-five, she married a free African American, John Tubman. In 1850, at the age of thirty, she made her escape.

A white neighbor sympathetic to the abolitionist cause slipped Harriet a piece of paper that told her where to find the nearest safe house. Once there, she was instructed to get into a wagon and hide under a sack. From there, she was taken north. She eventually escaped to Philadelphia, where she met William Still, the city's Underground Railroad station-master. Still took her under his wing, and Tubman soon joined the Underground Railroad.

Harriet Tubman would repeatedly risk her hard-won freedom by returning to the South as many as nineteen times to lead escaped slaves north. Among these fugitives were members of her own family, including her own parents. She escorted many of the former slaves to St. Catharines, in what was then called Upper Canada (now the province of Ontario). She is reported to have rescued more than 300 fugitives in her work with the Underground Railroad.

Tireless, determined, and courageous, Tubman became known as the Moses of her people, a comparison to the Jewish biblical hero who led his people out of slavery in Egypt. She was strong and had

Harriet Tubman helped hundreds of slaves escape to the North on the Underground Railroad. This photograph is believed to have been taken around 1880, long after the Civil War and emancipation.

incredible physical endurance. Many witnesses to her feats said she did not fear death at all and believed that God was watching over her. She carried a pistol for self-defense. She also carried small amounts of opium with her to help crying babies sleep so they would not endanger the mission. It is even said that Tubman considered shooting railroad "passengers" who expressed doubt and fear, wanting to turn back and return. "You'll be free or die!" she was rumored to say.

Like Moses, Tubman believed it was her divine mission to free her people. She was incredibly fortunate and kept her wits about her at all times. By the mid-1850s, there was a $40,000 reward for her capture, a small fortune at the time. When asked why she risked her life again and again, she would reply, "I can't die but once."

NOT SECURE EVEN IN THE NORTH

The flight of William and Ellen Craft is an example of the kind of ingenuity and daring required for slaves to flee their masters, escape to the North, and, once safely there, preserve their new and fragile freedom. Slaves on a Georgia plantation, the Crafts devised a very risky escape plan in 1848. Since Ellen was fair skinned, the couple decided that she would impersonate a slave owner and that he would act as her servant.

Ellen dressed as a young southern planter, right down to a stovepipe hat that was popular at the time. One giveaway, however, was Ellen's delicate, feminine features. To disguise them, she partially covered her face with a linen bandage to give the impression that she was suffering from a toothache. She also donned green eyeglasses to further mask her true identity. Since she had never been taught how to write, she put her arm in a sling so that her illiteracy could not be discovered. The plan called for

William, her "trusted servant," to do most of the talking and to shield them both from discovery.

The Crafts eventually arrived in Boston, Massachusetts, after passing through Charleston, South Carolina; Baltimore, Maryland; and Philadelphia, Pennsylvania. They received a hero's welcome in the antislavery capital, and people from all over the nation, even overseas, learned of their story. However, once they were living in the free North, their freedom was still not ensured.

The Crafts did not know they were being pursued by Georgia slave hunters, who had arrived in town to kidnap them and return them to the South. Word spread quickly among Boston's antislavery ranks, and the city's Vigilance Committee swept into action. The Vigilance Committees, formed in many cities where abolitionists lived, helped protect slaves who were escaping. They provided shelter, hiding places, and legal aid, and at times even defended fugitives with deadly force.

While Ellen Craft hid in the home of respected Boston lawyer William Loring in the nearby town of Brookline, William Craft stayed at the Hayden residence in Boston. William Lloyd Garrison came to visit Lewis Hayden and Craft and found the house

Ellen Craft, pictured here disguised as a man, and her husband, William, escaped a Georgia plantation. They fled to the North and on to England, where slavery had been abolished.

LEWIS HAYDEN

Many abolitionists were fully prepared to defend themselves and the fugitives they allowed into their homes. Among these was Lewis Hayden. Born into slavery in Kentucky in 1811, he was later sold to a Presbyterian minister. Hayden eventually decided that he could not live life as a slave. With his wife, Harriet, he fled Kentucky via the Underground Railroad. Living in Canada and then Detroit, Michigan, the Haydens eventually settled in Boston. There, they ran a clothing shop that doubled as a station on the Underground Railroad. They also harbored runaways in their home. It was at this time that the Haydens crossed paths with the famous fugitives William and Ellen Craft, who had just arrived in Boston.

Hayden risked his life to help the antislavery cause in Boston. When the Civil War broke out, he recruited soldiers for the Fifty-Fourth Regiment of the Massachusetts Volunteer Infantry, the first black regiment in the North. His son perished as a sailor in the Union navy. After the war, Hayden even became a state legislator in Massachusetts, providing an inspiring example to Americans of all races of how far someone could go who was offered the freedom and opportunity to succeed. After his death, his wife established a scholarship for needy black students entering Harvard Medical School.

barricaded like a fortress. Hayden's sons were on guard, sitting around a table piled with guns. According to most accounts, Hayden himself sat in the basement with two full kegs of gunpowder. The bounty hunters eventually came to the house. Hayden and his sons greeted their unwelcome guests at the door with lit candles, threatening to set off the gunpowder and blow everyone up should the slave catchers try to set foot in their home.

To add insult to injury, the slave hunters could not find a commissioner to serve the Crafts with a warrant for their arrest. Many Boston public officials sympathized with the abolitionists. Therefore, the bounty hunters could not recapture the Crafts under Massachusetts law. The Vigilance Committee also harassed the slave catchers at their hotel and on the streets, yelling "Slave hunters!" whenever they appeared. Frustrated, the Georgians eventually gave up and went home. After that, a priest legally married the Crafts, and they fled to England, where slavery had been abolished in 1833. In these unsafe times, no African American could be sure of his or her freedom anywhere in America, not even in the "free" North.

L. HAYDEN,
BOSTON

Lewis Hayden escaped slavery by way of the Underground Railroad. Once free, he ran an Underground Railroad station in his clothing store.

The Crafts were unwilling to take any more chances and fled to a new life across the Atlantic.

THE UNDERGROUND RAILROAD'S UNOFFICIAL PRESIDENT

Levi Coffin saw his first slave on a North Carolina road when he was seven. A group of slaves passed by, chained and handcuffed in a line, as Coffin stood near his father, who was chopping wood. He asked one of the men why they were chained and learned that the men had been captured from their families and enslaved. This incident opened the young boy's eyes to the evils of slavery, and from that moment on he strongly opposed it.

Born in 1798 in New Garden, North Carolina, Levi Coffin was a Quaker who became involved with the Underground Railroad and helped slaves escape to freedom. In 1826, Coffin, along with his wife, Catharine, and their children, moved to Newport, Indiana. There they ran a general store. For the next twenty years, the couple helped more than two thousand fugitives pass through the area on their way to the next "stop" on the railroad. The town became a central point on the Underground Railroad, with routes converging there from Madison and Jeffersonville, Indiana, and Cincinnati, Ohio. Not one of the escaped slaves they aided was ever recaptured. For his tireless efforts and his placement at an important crossroads on the railroad, Levi Coffin became known as the president of the Underground Railroad, even though there was no such official position.

After moving to Cincinnati, Ohio, the Coffins continued their work helping escaped slaves to freedom. Their house in Cincinnati was large and could accommodate many

Levi and Catharine Coffin stowed fugitive slaves in a compartment hidden under bags of grain in the wagon pictured above and transported them to the next Underground Railroad station.

fugitives. Some would hide upstairs for weeks without the knowledge of visitors or people who rented rooms there. Catharine Coffin often secretly took food hidden under fresh linens up to the slaves.

When the time seemed right, the Coffins hired horse teams to carry fugitives to the next station farther north, often about 30 miles (48 km) away. After dropping off their passengers, they would arrange for other Underground Railroad agents in that town to repeat the process.

BANKRUPT BUT STILL A BELIEVER

Another Quaker who fought against slavery was T http://www.shutterstock.com/subscribe.mhtml homas Garrett. Born a farmer's son in 1789, Garrett was an iron trader who settled in Wilmington, Delaware, a slave state. After joining the Pennsylvania Abolition Society, his home was soon known as the last stop on the Underground Railroad before the free state of Pennsylvania. It is estimated that more than two thousand runaways took shelter with Garrett during their flight north. Maryland authorities had a warrant for his arrest that offered a $10,000 reward.

In 1848, the law finally caught up with Garrett. A federal court charged him with aiding fugitives. Not only did Garrett refuse to deny the charge, he also declared that he would continue to help slaves escape to freedom. The court found him guilty and issued a fine that bankrupted him. Garrett's antislavery friends came to the rescue, however. With their financial help, he was able to restart his business.

Thanks to the efforts of agents like Tubman, Coffin, Garrett, and so many others, tens of thousands of slaves made the trip to free states and Canada. Without their help and the cooperation of all those working within the network, an estimated 100,000 slaves would have remained living under hopeless conditions.

CHAPTER FOUR

THE STRUGGLE BECOMES VIOLENT

B y the early nineteenth century, the two forces at odds over the issue of slavery struggled to get what they wanted. Those in favor of slavery believed that the system was absolutely necessary for maintaining the southern plantation economy, not to mention the southern culture they clung very strongly to. Abolitionists believed the country had a moral obligation to enforce the principles it was founded on.

The Missouri Compromise of 1820 was an attempt to strike a balance acceptable to both sides. The legislation deemed that all new states entering the Union would enter in pairs. A slave state could not be admitted without a free state also being admitted and vice versa. In addition, slavery would not be permitted in any new U.S. territories north of the latitude 36° 30'.

As an attempt to create peace between proslavery and antislavery forces, the Missouri Compromise failed. Rather than creating two separate but united groups of states—one slave, one free—the ongoing acceptance of slavery

This is a congressional conference committee report on the bill that would become known as the Missouri Compromise. (For a transcription, see page 52.)

that the compromise represented resulted in a wave of violence and bloodshed instead.

ORGANIZED VIOLENCE

Even as the Missouri Compromise was passed into law, trouble was brewing down south. In 1822, one of the most violent rebellions of the slavery era was being plotted in Charleston, South Carolina. Denmark Vesey, a charismatic and literate freeman, was planning a slave uprising.

Vesey recruited followers that numbered in the thousands. They made their own weapons, including bayonets and daggers. Their plan was to burn down Charleston and start a revolution against slavery. An informant betrayed their plans, however, before the operation could begin. Eventually, 130 of the conspirators were arrested. Twenty-two slaves were hanged along with Vesey.

More and more slaves were learning about the Underground Railroad and the possible trip north to freedom. It was becoming clear that the power of the slave owners was not absolute. The stage was set for further challenges to the masters and their social order. By 1831, the activities of the abolitionists and their Underground Railroad were making proslavery landowners increasingly nervous. Conspiracy theories and rumors of uprisings circulated widely.

NAT TURNER'S SLAVE REBELLION

That same year, Nat Turner would succeed where Denmark Vesey had failed.

Turner was a deeply religious slave from Southampton County, Virginia. He had taught himself to read and write and had recently come across an issue of the *Liberator*. He told other slaves that he had visions of black and white angels fighting in heaven. In August, he believed he had received a sign from God that the time was right to shed blood for freedom. He gathered seventy of his fellow men, stole guns, and went on a rampage.

During the next twenty-four hours, they massacred every white person they encountered, going from plantation to plantation in the surrounding area. Everywhere they marched, new recruits joined them. For many hours, they met no resistance, until armed patrols finally arrived. By then, the group had killed at least fifty-five men, women, and children. They scattered into the woods, and Nat Turner went into

HORRID MASSACRE IN VIRGINIA.

The Scenes which the above Plate is designed to represent are—Fig 1, a Mother intreating for the lives of her children.—2. Mr. Travis, cruelly murdered by his own Slaves.— 3. Mr. Barrow, who bravely defended himself until his wife escaped.—4. A comp. of mounted Dragoons in pursuit of the Blacks.

These 1831 illustrations show the massacre of whites by slaves during Nat Turner's rebellion.

hiding. After many weeks, Turner was found, tried for his crimes, and executed.

The Nat Turner rebellion was the single most powerful, violent revolt against slavery the country had ever seen. Blaming Turner's rebellious nature on his literacy, stricter laws were enacted to bar slaves from access to education. Any signs of disobedience were more harshly punished than ever before. The South began to look more and more like an armed camp, as militias were ordered to patrol plantation areas more frequently to prevent another such incident from happening.

ABOLITIONIST INTIMIDATION

Southern plantation owners were not the only Americans who favored slavery. In the North, merchants and laborers who depended on trade from the South were fiercely opposed to the threat of slavery's abolishment. Slavery made people money both south and north of the Mason-Dixon Line. When these businessmen and workers felt their livelihoods were being threatened, they often reacted with violence.

These attacks, designed to intimidate the antislavery forces, instead began to convince many people who had been neutral in their slavery views to embrace the abolitionist cause. In their eyes, the abolitionists were being assaulted for merely speaking their minds. The effort to halt the spread of antislavery sentiment resulted in many laws that Americans found to be oppressive. These included laws that prohibited the distribution of antislavery literature, which people felt was a violation of free speech.

A NEW FUGITIVE SLAVE ACT

In 1850, the U.S. Congress passed the controversial Fugitive Slave Law, an update of a similar bill passed in 1793. Southerners had argued that the loss of property through slave escapes to the North contributed to tremendous economic hardships. To stem their losses, slave owners would now have a law that made it easier to recapture their escaped slaves.

With the enactment of the Fugitive Slave Law of 1850, runaway slaves and free blacks were in greater danger

THE FUGITIVE SLAVE LAW.

The text of the Fugitive Slave Law is shown here in a broadside that was printed in Hartford, Connecticut, in 1850. (For a transcription, see pages 52–53.)

than ever before. Fugitives could now simply be identified by the affidavit of a slave hunter and forcibly taken south without any further proof or legal process. Runaways were not allowed trial by jury and could not speak in their own defense. Federal agents were now barred from preventing the capture of fugitives. It became a crime to hinder the capture of a slave in any way. Also, local police and other authorities were now required to help slave hunters in their work. The penalties for helping fugitives became harsher, with higher fines and more jail time.

Yet it was not only the roughly fifty thousand fugitives living in the North at the time who were in danger. Free blacks suddenly found themselves in jeopardy as well. Nothing could now prevent a slave hunter from kidnapping free men and women and, without any proof whatsoever, claiming them as fugitives.

The passage of the Fugitive Slave Law, far from restoring order as its supporters had hoped, only stoked the fire of the abolitionists' anger, resulting in a new wave of violent rebellions and uprisings.

BLOODY KANSAS AND JOHN BROWN

In 1854, Congress passed the Kansas-Nebraska Act. It was a direct repeal of the Missouri Compromise. Under this legislation, Congress left it to the voters in the Kansas and Nebraska Territories to decide whether they would enter the Union as free or slave states. The response to this act quickly turned violent. Antislavery and proslavery forces flocked to Kansas in an attempt to swing the vote their way. Slave owners and proslavery forces organized militias, and some tried to intimidate and influence voters at gunpoint.

In 1855, an abolitionist named John Brown entered Kansas Territory, where he joined his five sons. Brown was passionate about ending slavery. As a boy, he had seen a young black slave, a boy of twelve, beaten with a shovel. This, along with his father's extreme hatred of slavery, paved the way for his true life's work.

Brown had been very active in the Underground Railroad. He would hide fugitives in a secret basement that could be reached only through a hidden trap door in his tannery. Brown also served as a conductor on the railroad and would often escort fugitives from station to station. In these efforts, Brown often worked closely with Harriet Tubman.

During the height of tensions in the spring of 1856, proslavery forces burned the antislavery town of Lawrence to the ground. With four of his sons and two other followers, John Brown took his revenge. On the night of May 24, 1856, they reportedly dragged five unarmed proslavery settlers out of their beds near Osawatomie and hacked them to death with swords. Suddenly, Old Brown of Osawatomie, as John Brown was sometimes known, was a name that evoked dread and terror among the supporters of slavery.

Brown went on to plan and lead one of the most famous escapes in Underground Railroad history. In December 1858, a slave came to Brown and asked that he help him, his wife and children, and several other men to escape before being sold by their master and separated forever. Brown soon organized an expedition that marched on two estates and liberated the man and his family and the other slaves. From there, Brown and his men took the fugitives north to Canada.

John Brown grew a wild beard before his famous raid to disguise himself. The beard gave many the false impression that Brown was insane.

HARPERS FERRY

In 1859, Brown would set in motion the plan that he felt would achieve his destiny: bringing about the end of slavery in America. He had long planned to organize an armed revolt among slaves, starting in Virginia. He hoped

THE ADDRESS OF JOHN BROWN

The following is an excerpt of John Brown's address to the Virginia court before being given his death sentence for his raid on Harpers Ferry:

I have, may it please the Court, a few words to say. In the first place, I deny every thing but what I have already admitted, of a design on my part to free Slaves. I intended, certainly, to have made a clean thing of that matter, as I did last winter, when I went into Missouri, and there took slaves, without the snapping of a gun on either side, moving them through the country, and finally leaving them in Canada. I desired to have done the same thing again, on a much larger scale. That was all I intended. I never did intend murder, or treason, or the destruction of property, or to excite or incite Slaves to rebellion, or to make insurrection . . .

I believe that to have interfered as I have done, as I have always freely admitted I have done, in behalf of his [God's] despised poor, I have done no wrong, but right.

Now, if it is deemed necessary that I should forfeit my life, for the furtherance of the ends of justice, and mingle my blood further with the blood of my children, and with the blood of millions in this slave country, whose rights are disregarded by wicked, cruel, and unjust enactments—I say, let it be done.

this would create similar rebellions throughout the slave states. In the summer of that year, he moved his followers to Virginia and made his move on October 16, 1859. With twenty-one men, including five black men and four of his sons, Brown attacked and captured the U.S. armory and arsenal in the town of Harpers Ferry. Members of a Virginia militia and U.S. Marines surrounded Brown and stormed the building on October 18. Ten of Brown's men were killed in the fighting, and seven, including Brown, were captured. John Brown was found guilty of treason and hanged.

Brown became a powerful symbol of a nation coming apart at the seams. His violent death made antislavery radicals more impatient to rid the United States of slavery by any means necessary. And Brown's fiery moral passion and willingness to take action deeply frightened the proslavery forces, who now saw what lengths men would take to abolish the institution. People on both sides of the slavery issue saw Harpers Ferry as a troubling sign of things to come. A nation watched and waited for the impending storm.

Emotions regarding slavery were high everywhere, including among U.S. legislators. On May 22, 1856, Massachusetts senator Charles Sumner had been severely beaten on the floor of the Senate after expressing his disgust over the continuation of slavery and the power it held over the government. Indeed, the country's divide seemed to be deepening.

CHAPTER FIVE

THE CIVIL WAR AND THE UNDERGROUND RAILROAD

The 1850s marked the height of traffic escaping through the Underground Railroad. By this time, the United States was divided so deeply over the issue of slavery that it entered a period of great instability. On November 6, 1860, Republican Abraham Lincoln was elected president, and he wished nothing more than for the problem to go away so that he could be the leader of a united republic.

On December 20, 1860, South Carolina seceded from the Union, soon to be joined by Mississippi, Alabama, Florida, Georgia, Louisiana, and Texas. On April 12, 1861, troops loyal to the South fired on Fort Sumter, a military outpost off the coast of Charleston, South Carolina. And thus, the Civil War began. Within a few weeks, Arkansas, North Carolina, Tennessee, and Virginia also seceded, and this collection of states named itself the Confederate States of America, with Jefferson Davis, a southern politician, as its president.

This color-coded map from 1861 shows the division of the United States during that year. The states colored green seceded from the Union to create the Confederate States of America.

EXPANSION OF THE UNDERGROUND RAILROAD'S GOALS

By the time the Civil War was in full force, slaves were fleeing the South in droves. Shockingly, many of these fugitives were still unsafe even after they broke through the Union lines. Many Union officers allowed slave hunters to take these fugitives back. The Underground Railroad was needed more than ever.

AN UNDERGROUND RAILROAD IN EXISTENCE TODAY

The story of the Underground Railroad is powerful, but it is difficult to believe that such an escape network would be needed in modern times. However, there is an underground railroad similar to the one that helped fugitive slaves escape to freedom operating in Asia today.

North Koreans who are desperate to flee their nation's oppressive regime enlist the help of agents who shepherd them via a network of secret passages and safe houses to safety in China and Southeast Asia. The agents are often North Koreans who have successfully escaped, as well as members of Christian groups. Like those slaves who escaped and told their stories to abolitionist groups, many North Koreans who make it to safety provide information to the rest of the world about the horrors of the North Korean government.

But much like the risks encountered by fugitive slaves along their way, even once they reached free land, North Korean fugitives must worry about being discovered by the Chinese government. If returned home, they could face torture and imprisonment. As well, those agents who help North Koreans face criminal charges because it is illegal to engage in such activity in China.

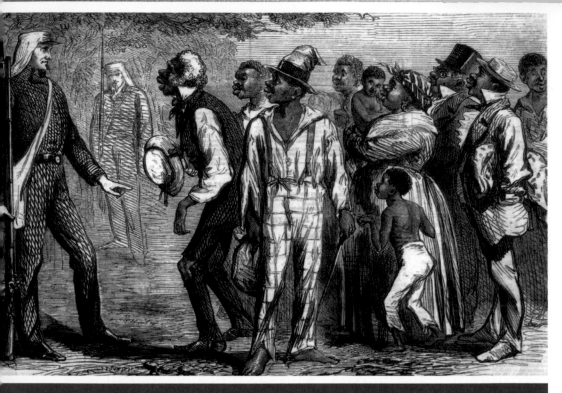

A group of runaway slaves is stopped at the Union lines during the Civil War. When the war started, many Underground Railroad agents shifted their efforts from sneaking a handful of escaped slaves north to handling a sudden and conspicuous flood of refugees.

Once the stream of fugitives from the South began to swell into the thousands, the Underground Railroad went "above ground" for the first time. What was once an escape route for a trickle of escaped slaves suddenly mushroomed into a refugee crisis. The agents of the railroad concentrated on the areas most used by the refugees who were escaping. Camps were set up, and volunteers helped feed and shelter the fugitives. Many volunteers also tended to those who had been wounded while escaping war-torn areas.

Harriet Tubman continued to be one of the greatest heroes of this era. She nursed and cooked for Union soldiers. She also aided blacks who were sick and hungry and had escaped into Union territory. Tubman even acted as a scout and spy for the Union army. She led raids into Confederate territories that she knew well.

Levi Coffin also worked hard for the new southern refugees fleeing slavery and war in the South. He became a leading member of the Western Freedmen's Aid Society after the Civil War. The society helped newly freed slaves by educating and teaching them how to earn a living, as well as assisting them in securing homes, food, and clothing when needed. Coffin traveled to England and other European countries and helped raise more than $100,000 for the society. He realized that one of the goals of the antislavery movement should be to work against the poverty and illiteracy that were the legacy of almost 250 years of slavery in America.

Other abolitionists and railroad agents chipped in in any way they could. Sojourner Truth, an African American woman, collected supplies for black regiments once they were allowed to fight in the Union army. After the Civil War, she even spoke on behalf of black Civil War veterans and helped them claim the land they had been promised for their participation.

This 1892 painting by Franklin Courter commemorates Sojourner Truth's meeting with President Abraham Lincoln, which took place at the White House on October 29, 1864.

FREEDOM

After the Union army won the bloody battle of Antietam, in Maryland, in September 1862, Lincoln used the victory to move forcefully in the direction of freedom for the slaves. On January 1, 1863, he issued the Emancipation Proclamation. It declared that all slaves within the Confederacy were now free. While the Union could not really enforce this proclamation, it was still a powerful symbolic move.

Lincoln's Emancipation Proclamation of 1863 declared that all slaves living in the Confederate states were free. (For a transcription, see pages 53–54.)

Many saw that the end of slavery was in sight and would be guaranteed with a Union victory over the Confederacy.

By the end of 1864, the South had run out of money and the will to fight. Its armies were retreating. On April 9, 1865, the commander of the Confederate army, General Robert. E. Lee, surrendered to General Ulysses S. Grant of the Union army at Appomattox, Virginia, ending the War between the States.

By December 1865, Congress had ratified the Lincoln-supported Thirteenth Amendment to the U.S. Constitution, which outlawed slavery throughout the nation. The Fourteenth Amendment,

which followed in 1868, granted citizenship to all former slaves. The seemingly unreachable goal of freedom
for all African Americans had finally been achieved. The
abolitionists' victory took a long time but was stunning
nevertheless. With the invaluable help of the Underground Railroad, slavery had become a shameful thing
of the past in America.

The history of the Underground Railroad is distinguished
by great creativity, courage, endurance, and faith. Its agents
helped many thousands to live in freedom for the first time
in their lives. The railroad's successes, and even its failures,
helped to rally millions of other Americans against slavery
and turn the tide against the institution. The truth is, change
did not happen immediately. The abolition of slavery did
not mean that black Americans were treated as equal to
white Americans. Although slavery was abolished, the U.S.
government would resume its practice of institutional racism, enacting laws that effectively discriminated against
African Americans. The civil rights movement of the 1950s
and 1960s went a long way toward equality, but even today,
the road to true equality remains a challenging one. Yet the
bravery and fortitude of the agents of the Underground
Railroad and those who used it to escape to better lives are
examples of the spirit of the United States imagined by the
Founding Fathers.

TIMELINE

1619 Twenty Africans are shipped to Jamestown, Virginia, on Dutch ships. They are the first slaves imported into Britain's North American colonies.

1642 The Virginia Colony issues fines to those who hide or otherwise help runaway slaves.

1741 The North Carolina Colony passes laws allowing for the prosecution of any persons caught assisting runaway slaves.

1775 The world's first abolitionist society is founded by Anthony Benezet to protect runaway slaves and free blacks who were illegally captured and enslaved.

1777 Vermont becomes the first U.S. territory to abolish slavery.

1777–1804 All northern states abolish slavery.

1780 Pennsylvania becomes the first state to abolish slavery.

1793 The Fugitive Slave Act becomes a federal law and allows slave owners and their agents to seize runaway slaves, even in free states and territories. Any efforts to prevent the capture of fugitives are outlawed and punishable.

1804 The Underground Railroad is unofficially inaugurated after slave owner General Thomas Boudes of Columbia, Pennsylvania, refuses to release escaped slaves to authorities.

1818 Abolitionists begin using the Underground Railroad to help slaves escape to Canada through Ohio.

1820 The Missouri Compromise allows Missouri to enter the Union as a slave state, while Maine enters as a free state. It also outlaws slavery in any new states or territories north of the latitude 36° 30'.

1830 Levi Coffin leaves North Carolina, settles in Indiana, and resumes his Underground Railroad activities.

1831 William Lloyd Garrison prints the first issue of the antislavery newspaper the *Liberator*.

1838 The Underground Railroad is formally organized. Black abolitionist Robert Purvis becomes chairman of the General Vigilance Committee and "president" of the Underground Railroad, a title that Levi Coffin would also unofficially hold.

1849 Harriet Tubman escapes from her owner in Maryland. She will return to the South at least nineteen times to help rescue several hundred other slaves.

1850 In exchange for agreeing to allow California to enter the Union as a free state, the harsher Fugitive Slave Act is passed.

1857 The U.S. Supreme Court decides, in *Scott v. Sandford*, that blacks can never be citizens, that Congress cannot outlaw slavery in any U.S. territory, and that slaveholders can take slaves even in free areas of the country.

1860 Republican candidate Abraham Lincoln is elected president of the United States.

1861 The Civil War begins.

1863 President Lincoln issues the Emancipation Proclamation, freeing all slaves throughout the United States.

1865 The Civil War ends. The Thirteenth Amendment abolishes slavery in the United States permanently.

SAYVILLE LIBRARY

PAGE 34: EXCERPT FROM THE CONGRESSIONAL CONFERENCE COMMITTEE REPORT ON THE PROPOSED MISSOURI COMPROMISE OF 1820

And be it further enacted. That in all that territory ceded by France to the United States, under the name of Louisiana, which lies north of thirty-six degrees and thirty minutes north latitude, not included within the limits of the state, contemplated by this act, slavery and involuntary servitude, otherwise than in the punishment of crimes, whereof the parties shall have been duly convicted, shall be, and is hereby, forever prohibited: Provided always, That any person escaping into the same, from whom labour or service is lawfully claimed, in any state or territory of the United States, such fugitive may be lawfully reclaimed and conveyed to the person claiming his or her labour or service as aforesaid.

CONTEMPORARY ENGLISH TRANSLATION

In all the territory of the Louisiana Purchase north of the latitude 36°30′ and not part of the Missouri Territory described in this act, slavery will be illegal (though people convicted of crimes will continue to be arrested and held in prison). Slaves who escape to this territory or any other state in the Union, however, can be caught and returned to their masters.

PAGE 38: EXCERPT FROM THE FUGITIVE SLAVE LAW OF 1850 (PART OF THE COMPROMISE OF 1850)

7. Resolved, That more effectual provision ought to be made by law, according to the requirement of the Constitution, for the restitution and delivery of persons bound to service or labor in any State, who may escape into any other State or Territory in the Union. And,

8. Resolved, That Congress has no power to promote or obstruct the trade in slaves between the slaveholding States; but that the admission

or exclusion of slaves brought from one into another of them, depends exclusively upon their own particular laws.

CONTEMPORARY ENGLISH TRANSLATION

7. It is decided that, as required by the Constitution, a stronger law must be passed to require the return of escaped slaves to their masters, regardless of what state they have fled from and which state or territory they have fled to.

8. It is also decided that Congress has no right to get involved in the buying and selling of slaves that occurs between the slave states. Instead, the laws of each slave state must determine whether trading in slaves with other slave states is forbidden or allowed.

PAGE 48: EXCERPT FROM THE EMANCIPATION PROCLAMATION

By the President of the United States of America:
A Proclamation.
Whereas, on the twenty-second day of September, in the year of our Lord one thousand eight hundred and sixty-two, a proclamation was issued by the President of the United States, containing, among other things, the following, to wit:
"That on the first day of January, in the year of our Lord one thousand eight hundred and sixty-three, all persons held as slaves within any State or designated part of a State, the people whereof shall then be in rebellion against the United States, shall be then, thenceforward, and forever free; and the Executive Government of the United States, including the military and naval authority thereof, will recognize and maintain the freedom of such persons, and will do no act or acts to repress such persons, or any of them, in any efforts they may make for their actual freedom."

CONTEMPORARY ENGLISH TRANSLATION

On September 22, 1862, the president of the United States issued a proclamation that said this, among other things:

"Beginning January 1, 1863, all people being held as slaves in any of the rebelling states will be considered free, forever. The U.S. Government, including the army and navy, will recognize, enforce, and protect the freedom of these ex-slaves and will do nothing to prevent their attempts to gain their freedom."

GLOSSARY

abolitionist Someone who works to end slavery.

conductor A person who escorted fugitive slaves from station to station on the Underground Railroad.

emancipation Freedom from slavery or some other controlling, restrictive influence.

fugitive A person who has escaped and fled.

institutional racism In the United States, laws, systems, and social structures that marginalize people of color and provide distinct advantages to white people.

martyr A person who dies for a cause.

memoir A narrative that tells the tale of all or part of one's life.

overseer The person in charge of guarding and punishing slaves.

peculiar institution A term southerners used for slavery, both because they felt the institution was singular to them and also because the term was less crass than the word "slavery."

plantation Huge farm in the southern United States, mostly worked by slave labor before the Civil War.

Quakers Members of a religious group, many of whom were against slavery and helped with the Underground Railroad.

secede To quit or withdraw from.

station A stop on the Underground Railroad where fugitive slaves were hidden.

stationmaster The person who sheltered fugitives at his or her stop on the Underground Railroad.

Buxton National Historic Site and Museum
North Buxton Chatham
Ontario, Canada
(519) 352-4799
Website: http://www.buxtonmuseum.com
This museum commemorates the Underground Railroad
and is a tribute to the Elgin Settlement, which harbored
fugitive and free African Americans.

Charles Wright Museum of African American History
315 E. Warren Avenue
Detroit, MI 48201-1443
(313) 494-5800
Website: http://www.maah-detroit.org
The Charles H. Wright Museum of African American History
hosts The Underground Railroad: The Struggle Against
Slavery, a robust online portal designed to facilitate a
greater awareness of the history of the Underground
Railroad.

Harriet Tubman Museum and Educational Center
424 Race Street
Cambridge, MD 21613-1836
(410) 228-0401
Website: http://www.harriettubmanbyway.org
Exhibits and resources are available during hours of operation.
Step-on guided tours of area sites associated with Harriet
Tubman are available by appointment. A gift shop and
literature about area attractions are also available.

John Freeman Walls Historic Site and Underground
Railroad Museum
Lakeshore

Windsor, Ontario, Canada
(519) 727-6555
Website: http://www.undergroundrailroadmuseum.org
This site was an endpoint on the Underground Railroad
   and a place where escaped slaves began new lives. It is
   available for tour three months of the year.

National Underground Railroad Freedom Center
312 Elm Street, Suite 1250
Cincinnati, OH 45202
(513) 412-6900
Website: http://www.freedomcenter.org
The National Underground Railroad Freedom Center
   reveals stories about freedom's heroes, from the era
   of the Underground Railroad to contemporary times,
   challenging and inspiring everyone to take courageous
   steps for freedom today.

North Star Underground Railroad Museum
1131 Mace Chasm Road
Ausable Chasm, NY 12911
(518) 834-5180
Website: http://www.northcountryundergroundrailroad.com
This museum brings to life the struggle for freedom as it
   played out in the Lake Champlain/Adirondack region. It
   highlights stories of escaped slaves and the local people
   who helped them.

Underground Railroad Foundation
121 East Hight Street
Flushing, OH 43977
(740) 968-2080
Website: http://www.ugrrf.org

The Underground Railroad Museum features an extensive collection of publications, books, memorabilia, and other articles. The exhibits portray what is known about slavery and the Underground Railroad in Ohio and features an understanding of the culture in the 1800s.

WEBSITES

Because of the changing nature of Internet links, the Rosen Publishing Group, Inc., has developed an online list of websites related to the subject of this book. This site is updated regularly. Please use this link to access the list:

http://www.rosenlinks.com/UAH/Under

FOR FURTHER READING

Adler, David A. *Harriet Tubman and the Underground Railroad.* New York, NY: Holiday House, 2012.

Ayres, Katherine. *North by Night: A Story of the Underground Railroad.* New York, NY: Random House Children's Books, 2000.

Brill, Marlene Targ. *The Underground Railroad Adventure of Allen Jay, Antislavery Activist.* N. Minneapolis, MN: Lerner Books, 2011.

Chipley-Slavicek, Louise. *Harriet Tubman and the Underground Railroad.* Farmington Hills, MI: Lucent Books, 2006.

Edwards, Judith. *Abolitionists and Slave Resistance.* Berkeley Heights, NJ: Enslow, 2004.

Jordan, Anne Devereaux. *Slavery and Resistance.* New York, NY: Cavendish Square, 2006.

Lassieur, Allison. *The Underground Railroad.* North Mankato, MN: Capstone Press, 2014.

Lawing, Charlie B. *William Lloyd Garrison and the Liberator* (World Writers). Greensboro, NC: Morgan Reynolds, Inc., 1999.

McKissack, Patricia C. *A Picture of Freedom: The Diary of Clotee, a Slave Girl, Belmont Plantation, Virginia, 1859.* New York, NY: Scholastic, 2011.

McNeese, Tim. *The Abolitionist Movement.* New York, NY: Chelsea House, 2007.

Northup, Solomon. *Twelve Years a Slave.* Start Publishing, 2013.

Painter, Nell Irvin. *Sojourner Truth: A Life, a Symbol.* New York, NY: W. W. Norton & Company, 1997.

Rappaport, Doreen. *Escape from Slavery: Five Journeys to Freedom.* New York, NY: Harper Trophy, 1999.

Sawyer, Kem Knapp. *The Amazing Underground Railroad.* Berkeley Heights, NJ: Enslow, 2013.

Schraff, Anne. *Frederick Douglass: Speaking Out Against Slavery.* Berkeley Heights, NJ: Enslow Publishers, Inc., 2002.

Stein, R. Conrad. *Escaping Slavery on the Underground Railroad.* Berkeley Heights, NJ: Enslow, 2008.

Stowe, Harriet Beecher. *Uncle Tom's Cabin* (Young Folk's Edition). SMK Books, 2011.

Truth, Sojourner. *Narrative of Sojourner Truth.* New York, NY: HarperCollins, 2014.

BIBLIOGRAPHY

Blockson, Charles L. "Escape from Slavery: The Underground Railroad." *National Geographic*, July 1984, pp. 3–39.

Blockson, Charles L. *Hippocrene Guide to the Underground Railroad.* New York, NY: Hippocrene Books, 1994.

Blockson, Charles L. *The Underground Railroad: Dramatic Firsthand Accounts of Daring Escapes to Freedom.* New York, NY: Berkley Books, 1987.

Buckmaster, Henrietta. *Flight to Freedom: The Story of the Underground Railroad.* New York, NY: Thomas Y. Crowell Company, 1958.

Jacobs, Donald M., ed. *Courage and Conscience: Black and White Abolitionists in Boston.* Indianapolis, IN: Indiana University Press, 1993.

Radio Free Asia. "Escape from North Korea." Retrieved October 28, 2014 (http://www.rfa.org/english/commentaries/freedom-01032013175723.html).

Tobin, Jacqueline, et al. *Hidden in Plain View: A Secret Story of Quilts and the Underground Railroad.* New York, NY: Bantam, 2000.

Walls, Bryan. "Henry 'Box' Brown: Freedom Marker: Courage and Creativity." Retrieved October 28, 2014 (http://www.pbs.org/black-culture/shows/list/underground-railroad/stories-freedom/henry-box-brown).

INDEX

ABOUT THE AUTHORS

Philip Wolny is a writer from Queens, New York. His other historical titles for Rosen Publishing include *Gun Rights: Interpreting the Constitution* and *Colonialism: A Primary Source Analysis.*

Viola Jones is a teacher and writer who specializes in making U.S. history interesting to young adults.

PHOTO CREDITS

Cover, pp. 10, 36 MPI/Archive Photos/Getty Images; p. 3 Lone Wolf Photography/Shutterstock.com; pp. 4–5 (background) Enigmangels/Shutterstock.com; p. 5 (inset) © North Wind Picture Archives/Alamy; pp. 7, 14, 24, 33, 43 Everett Historical/Shutterstock.com; pp. 9, 38 Library of Congress Rare Book and Special Collections Division; p. 12 adapted from the National Park Service map of escape routes of the Underground Railroad, NPS cartographic staff at Harpers Ferry Center; pp. 15, 23 © AP Images; p. 19 © Pat Canova/Alamy; pp. 20, 25, 40 Library of Congress Prints and Photographs Division; p. 27 courtesy North Carolina Central University; p. 29 courtesy of the Museum of Afro-American History; p. 31 courtesy of Levi Coffin House Association and WayNet.org; pp. 34, 48 National Archives and Records Administration; p. 44 Private Collection/Bridgeman Images; p. 46 © Interfoto/Alamy; p. 47 Courtesy of the Archive of the Historical Society of Battle Creek; cover, p. 1 design elements Piotr Krzeslak/Shutterstock.com (flag), Aleksandrs Bondars/Shutterstock.com (scroll); cover and interior pages background textures chudo-yudo/Shutterstock.com, Alina G/Shutterstock.com, Attitude/Shutterstock.com, sl_photo/Shutterstock.com

Designer: Michael Moy; Editor: Christine Poolos

Sayville Library
88 Greene Avenue
Sayville, NY 11782

JUN 0 8 2016

DISCARDED BY
SAYVILLE LIBRARY